People Jesus Met

by

B. A. Ramsbottom

GOSPEL STANDARD TRUST
PUBLICATIONS
1991
7 Brackendale Grove, Harpenden,
Herts. AL5 3EL, England.

John the Baptist

Crowds of people were going out into the wilderness. See them leaving their homes. Some were coming from the great city of Jerusalem. Some were coming from the little towns. Some were bad, unkind people. Some were people who thought they were good. Some were soldiers. There were all sorts of people.

What were they doing? And why were they going into a wilderness? A wilderness is a place where no one lives. Not much grows there. The ground is hard and rocky. What did they want?

They were going to see a man named John. We usually call him "John the Baptist." They wanted to listen to him.

I wonder if the people were surprised when they saw John for the first time? He was quite young but he had long hair and a long beard. He wore very rough clothes (they were made out of hair from camels) and round him he had a leather belt. He lived all alone out in the wilderness. The only thing he could find to eat was honey (which the bees made in the rocks) and little flying creatures called locusts (which he caught).

But John was a good man. He was a man of God. And as he preached the people listened. He told them they were sinful. He told them God was angry and that they needed to repent — to be sorry for their sins and to leave them. All of us need to repent. May we ask God to give us repentance.

Now watch what John is doing! See him taking these people out into the River Jordan (which flowed nearby) and dipping them underneath the water. He is baptizing them. Not everybody! Only those who were really sorry for their sins.

Then one day the Lord Jesus Himself came to see John. He too asked John to baptize Him. At first John said "No"; he was not good enough to baptize Jesus his Lord and Master. And he could not understand why Jesus wanted to be baptized; He was not a sinner. But then John did as Jesus asked him.

But now what wonderful things happened! As John was lifting up the Lord out of the water, a beautiful dove came down and lighted on His head. It was not an ordinary dove. It was the Holy Spirit coming from heaven like a dove. And then a voice could be heard speaking from heaven — the voice of God the Father. It said, "This is My beloved Son, in whom I am well pleased."

Another day, as John was preaching, the Lord Jesus came again. John was so pleased. He looked at Jesus and cried, "Behold the Lamb of God!" What a lovely name for the Lord Jesus, "the Lamb of God!" A Lamb — so gentle and tender, so pure, but a Lamb who one day would be killed.

The people began to leave John and go with Jesus. But John was very happy. He loved the Lord Jesus dearly.

And the Lord Jesus dearly loved John. Do you know what He said about him? That of all the people who had ever lived, there had never been a greater man than John the Baptist.

You can read about this in Matthew chapter 3; Mark chapter 1, verses 1 to 11; Luke chapter 3, verses 1 to 22; John chapter 1, verses 29 to 37.

Ask God to give you grace to repent and to believe on the Lord Jesus. Only those who repent and believe are forgiven.

The Woman at the Well

One day Jesus was very, very tired. Did you know that Jesus sometimes felt tired, just as we do? You see, He was a real Man though He was Almighty God.

The Lord Jesus was on a long journey. It was the middle of the day when the sun was really hot. As well as feeling tired, He was thirsty. I wonder if you have felt really thirsty? So He sat down to have a rest on a well. It was a famous well called "Jacob's Well."

As He sat there a woman came along to the well. She was carrying a waterpot so she could draw water. Probably she would be carrying it on her head.

Now this woman was a bad woman. And though she did not realize it, Jesus knew how bad she was and the bad things she did. The Lord Jesus knows all about each one of us.

Jesus asked this woman if He could have a drink of water. She was very surprised but she began to talk to Him.

But soon she realized that there was something different about the Lord Jesus. She began to think He must be a prophet. How could it be that He knew all about her? She had never seen Him before.

Then He began to talk about giving her what He

called "living water." Whatever could He mean? He had no bucket or waterpot and the well was very deep. She was bewildered.

What did He mean? Really Jesus meant this. God's blessings are like a drink of lovely cool water to those who are thirsty. May the Holy Spirit teach us what "living water" is so that we thirst for it.

When the woman found out that Jesus knew all about her bad ways, and that He was a prophet, she thought she would talk to Him about all sorts of things, and ask Him all sorts of questions. Perhaps she wanted to change the subject.

In the end she cried out, "When the Messiah, the Son of God, comes to this world, He will be able to tell us the answer to all these questions."

What a surprise she got! Jesus said, "I am He."

Really the Lord Jesus made Himself known to this poor, sinful woman more clearly than to anyone else He met. What must she have felt?

You see, Jesus loved her. He found her out. He showed her her need. He forgave her. She would no longer live a wicked life now.

Do you know what she did? She told everyone about this wonderful Person she had met. And do you know what else? She forgot all about her waterpot. She left it at the well. She had got something better.

You can read this story in John chapter 4, verses 1 to 42.

Ask the Lord Jesus to teach you what "living water" is.

The Woman in Simon's House

When Jesus was here on earth, there were some people who did not like Him. They were His enemies. They were called Pharisees. They thought they were very good — but really they weren't. They did not like Jesus because He told them about the bad things they did.

But one day one of these Pharisees asked Jesus to go for dinner. His name was Simon.

We wonder why he asked Jesus to his house. Well, we do not know. But we know that when Jesus arrived, he did not treat Him very kindly. In Bible days, if a person came to your house, you always washed his feet with water (people's feet got very hot and dusty) — but Simon did not.

Anyway, the meal began. They started to eat and talk. But who is this? And what is she doing? She is a woman everyone knows; she has been a very bad woman. However did she get in?

But watch her! She is crying — she feels so sorry about the bad things she has done — and she cries so much that her tears fall on Jesus' feet. Now she bends down and begins to dry them with her long hair. Now she is kissing them. How much she must love the Lord Jesus! But now she is pouring beautifully smelling ointment over His feet to cool and refresh them.

Simon watched with amazement. But he was not very pleased. He also began to think some very unkind thoughts. He thought, "Everyone says Jesus is a prophet. He can't be — or He would have known who this woman is. She is a sinner."

Now Jesus knew everything Simon was thinking. Did you know that He knows everything that you think? No one else can know, but Jesus does.

Then Jesus told a little story. Once there was a man with a lot of money. He lent some of it to two different people; they would have to give it back to him. But to one he gave 50 pennies and to the other ten times as much, 500 pennies.

When the time came for them to give him his money back, they couldn't. They had spent it. They had not one penny left. Now they could have been sent to prison, couldn't they? But the man was very, very kind. He said, "I will let you off." They must have been very, very glad. What a nice story!

But then Jesus turned to Simon. He asked him a question, "Simon, which of these two do you think would love the man most?"

It was an easy question. Of course, the man who had been let off the 500 pennies he owed. Quickly Simon answered.

But why was Jesus telling this little story? Simon soon knew.

Jesus turned and said, "Simon, you never washed

My feet. This woman has washed them with her tears, and wiped them with her long hair. You never kissed Me. This woman kissed My feet. You didn't anoint My head with ointment; this woman has anointed My feet. That is why I told the story. She has had many, many sins forgiven — so she loves Me very, very much."

Only Jesus can forgive sins. So He said to the woman, "Thy sins are forgiven." How happy she must have been! She went away with her heart full of peace — a loving follower of the Lord Jesus.

You can read this story in Luke chapter 7, verses 36 to 50.

We too need forgiving. And no one can forgive us but the Lord Jesus. There is a beautiful word: "If we confess our sins, He is faithful and just to forgive us our sins, and to cleanse us from all unrighteousness."

The Scribe

One day an important looking man came up to Jesus. He was called a scribe. Now most of the scribes did not like Jesus. But this one spoke very, very kindly to Him. He said he would like to be with Jesus — always. He promised that he would never leave Him, whatever happened.

We should have thought that Jesus would have been very happy to have this important man serving Him, shouldn't we? But Jesus was not happy. He knew what this man really was like. He knew he would soon grow tired of being a follower of Jesus. Jesus knows all about us. He knows what we are really like. He even knows what we are thinking — because He is God.

So Jesus told the scribe a little story. Have you ever seen what the little birds do at the end of the day? They fly back to their warm nests, and there they are safe and comfortable all night. And even the foxes! Have you ever seen a fox? They are beautiful creatures, with long bushy tails, but they are very cruel. Yet even they have their homes where they can sleep warmly and comfortably at night — holes in the earth.

Now said Jesus, "I have no home of My own!" Think of it! The Lord Jesus made all things, yet He did not have any home of His own. Sometimes He

had to stay out all night long on the cold hills and mountains.

What Jesus really meant was this: If you follow Me, it will not be so easy as you think. It will not just be watching Me doing miracles. It will not just be crowds of people gathering round. It will be hard. Those who followed Jesus when He was here on earth knew much sadness.

And do you know? The scribe did not say a single word. He had nothing to say. And we never hear of him again. The cost of following Jesus was too much for him.

You know, the Lord Jesus once said, "If any man will come after Me, let him deny himself, and take up his cross, and follow Me." May we be true followers of Jesus.

You can read this story in Matthew chapter 8, verses 19 and 20 and in Luke chapter 9, verses 57 and 58.

That is a good little prayer:
"As the birds seek their shelter, and all tired things their resting places, so may we ever seek Thee, Lord Jesus, at the close of this and every day. Amen."

The Ten Lepers

These are strange people Jesus is meeting! There are ten of them altogether. They look thin and ill. Their skin is rough and looks dirty. Even their fingers are beginning to drop off. Yes, they are lepers. What a dreadful thing it was to be a leper!

They are not allowed to go near to anyone. But, listen, what a noise they are making! What is it they are saying?

"Master, have mercy on us."

They know Jesus can make them better — if only He will. So they cry for mercy.

It was a strange thing that Jesus told them to do. He told them to go to the priest and show themselves to him. But that was what a leper must do only if he had been made better. And these lepers were still full of leprosy.

Anyway, they did as they were told. And as they went, one by one they suddenly realized they were better. How happy they must have been! Yes, it was the Lord Jesus who had made them better; their skin now was like the skin of anyone else.

So gladly they hurried on their way. But what is happening? One of them is turning back. Has he forgotten something? Why, he is singing praises to God and thanking Him for all He has done.

Reaching the Lord Jesus, he falls down flat at His

feet. What love is in his heart and how he worships the Lord Jesus! He cannot thank Him enough for His kindness.

And how strange! This one who remembered to give thanks was not even one of God's people, the Jews. He was a Samaritan — whom no one likes.

Jesus was very, very pleased. He always is when we thank Him for His mercies. But He asked a question: "Where are the other nine?" It was sad that they were so ungrateful. But before He sent him away the Lord Jesus spoke some very kind words to the one who had come back.

We too need healing — because we have sinned against God and are like lepers before Him. O! but if the Lord Jesus cleanses us with His precious blood, let us be thankful.

You can read this story in Luke chapter 17, verses 11 to 19.

A good prayer: "Cleanse me from my sin."

Zacchaeus

There was once a very little man called Zacchaeus. He had lots of money but, sadly, he was not a good man. He was very greedy. He was very unkind.

But one day he heard that Jesus was visiting the town where he lived, Jericho. So he thought he would like to see Him. Perhaps he had heard of all the wonderful things that Jesus had done. But just why he wanted to see Him, we do not really know.

Anyway, he went. But there were crowds of people and Zacchaeus was so small that he just could not see over their heads. (Some of you little ones will know what that is — you have been among a lot of people, and you were so small, you could not see anything.)

But what do you think little Zacchaeus did? He climbed up a tree and sat comfortably in its branches. It was a good idea wasn't it? The little man wasn't going to give up very easily. But the people must have been amazed to see him sitting up in a tree, mustn't they?

At last the time Zacchaeus was waiting for arrived. And there for the first time he saw the Lord Jesus. But what is happening? Someone is calling his name: "Zacchaeus." It is Jesus Himself.

What a shock this must have been! How did Jesus know his name?

But now Jesus tells him to be quick and climb down from the tree. He wants to come to Zacchaeus' house.

So as quickly as he could, Zacchaeus came down and took Jesus home with him.

But the people just could not understand why. They started to grumble. "Why has He gone with Zacchaeus? Does He not know that he is a wicked little man?"

Of course Jesus did! But He was going to change the life of the little man. Can you remember? Jesus said, "I came not to call the righteous, but sinners to repentance."

Zacchaeus began to realize how wicked he had been. He was really sorry. And he meant it — and he wanted to show it. He said, "Lord, I will give half of my goods to the poor." (He knew that Jesus was the Lord.) All those he had treated unkindly he now wanted to help. Those he had taken money from, he wanted to give them four times as much back. How pleased they would be!

What a change had taken place! What a different man little Zacchaeus was! How can we explain it? Well, Jesus Himself said, "Today is salvation come to thy house." Jesus had saved him — and when He saves it is for ever.

Do you know why He is called Jesus ("THE SAVIOUR")? Because "He shall save His people from their sins."

You can read this story in Luke chapter 19, verses 1 to 10.

May the Holy Spirit teach you your need of being saved from your sins. That is a good little prayer, "LORD, SAVE ME."

The Children of Jerusalem

Some of the people Jesus met were children. This story is about the children of Jerusalem.

At the end of His life the Lord Jesus rode into Jerusalem on a donkey. He was on His way to die on the cross. Crowds of people threw their clothes on the road (to make a carpet for Him). Others cut down branches from the trees and waved them. People shouted, "Hosanna! Hosanna!"

Jesus went along to the temple in Jerusalem. It was like a large church or chapel. It was God's house. But there, inside, were all kinds of people selling things. Jesus was angry. We often think of "Gentle Jesus, meek and mild" (don't we?); but never forget, Jesus is angry with sin. But now watch what He did! Suddenly He threw the tables of those who were selling things on to the floor, and knocked over their seats, and drove them out.

Afterwards very kindly He made sick people better. There were some who were blind, and He made them see. There were others who were lame, and He made them walk.

But now look! There are young children there. And Jesus was pleased to see them. They cried out "Hosanna" to Him. Little children in Jerusalem were taught to cry "Hosanna" to God — but who told them to cry "Hosanna" to Jesus? They called

Him "the Son of David" — the one who should come, God's dear Son.

When Jesus rode on the donkey into Jerusalem, we are told that all the people were asking the question, "WHO IS THIS?" Well, these little children in the temple knew the answer. They knew who Jesus is. They knew that He is the Son of God. They worshipped Him. They cried, "Hosanna!"

Do you know who Jesus is? Can you answer the question everyone was asking?

But how sad! The priests and the scribes were angry. They did not love the Lord Jesus and they did not like to hear these little ones crying "Hosanna" to Him.

So they complained. They went up to Jesus and told Him to stop them. But He didn't. He said that God had promised that little ones, even babies, would praise Him. And He said that it was God who had taught them.

Not one of us is too young to be taught by God. How wonderful that among those Jesus met were little children!

You can read this story in Matthew chapter 21, verses 1 to 16. See also Psalm 8.

Pray that the Lord Jesus will show you *what you are* and *who He is.*

Mary Magdalene

There was one woman who specially loved the Lord Jesus. Her name was Mary Magdalene. She had once been a wicked woman but Jesus had forgiven her. That is why she loved Him so much. She left her old bad ways and now liked to be with Jesus.

You have all heard how Jesus died on the cross, and then He was buried in the grave.

But now, who is that standing by the grave, crying? It is Mary Magdalene. She is crying bitterly. She is so sad because her Lord and Master, Jesus, has died such a cruel death.

But soon she is going to have the most wonderful surprise of her life. Though she does not know it, Jesus is no longer dead. He is alive. If only Mary knew!

But there she is, still crying. And she looks inside the grave. What can she see? Two holy angels dressed in white — and they speak to her. They ask her why she is crying. Wouldn't you and I be pleased if two angels came and talked to us? But Mary was not. She only wanted Jesus.

Now the grave was in a garden. And in that garden the Lord Jesus was standing, watching Mary. How dearly He loved her!

Suddenly Mary Magdalene turned round — and

there she saw Jesus. But she did not recognize Him. Perhaps it was because her eyes were full of tears. Or perhaps He did not look the same. She thought it was only the man who looked after the flowers and trees in the garden — the gardener.

The gardener kindly asked her what she wanted and why she was crying.

"O!" she said, "have you taken Him away? Please tell me where you have put Him." She did not know she was talking to Jesus.

Then, unexpectedly, she heard a voice calling her name. It was saying, "Mary." It was the voice of Jesus. But how could it be? It was the gardener that was speaking.

Then suddenly she knew. That man was not the gardener; He *was* the Lord Jesus. O how sweet that voice was to her! She had never heard anything so lovely. Then Jesus must be alive.

Immediately she turned and said to Him, "Rabboni — my dearest Master."

How wonderful that of all Jesus' friends and followers, it was to Mary Magdalene that He came first of all after He had come back to life! She was the happiest woman on earth. No more tears now — she is happy.

What do you think she did? She hurried as quickly as she could and told Jesus' disciples. She said, "I have seen the Lord."